Tadpole Books are published by Jump!, 5357 Penn Avenue South, Minneapolis, MN 55419, www.jumplibrary.com

Copyright ©2019 Jump!. International copyright reserved in all countries. No part of this book may be reproduced in any form without written permission from the publisher.

Editor: Jenna Trnka **Designer:** Anna Peterson **Translator:** Annette Granat

Photo Credits: Sonsedska Yuliia/Shutterstock, cover, 6–7, 8–9, 16tr, 16bm; Eric Isselee/Shutterstock, 1; Diana Carpenter/Shutterstock, 2–3, 16bl; Jeff Stamer/Shutterstock, 4–5, 16tm; Heiko Kiera/Shutterstock, 10–11, 16br; Dssimages/Dreamstime, 12–13; jimkruger/iStock, 14–15 (foreground); Zack Frank/Shutterstock, 14–15 (background), 16btl.

Library of Congress Cataloging-in-Publication Data
Names: Nilsen, Genevieve, author.
Title: Los kits / por Genevieve Nilsen.
Other titles: Raccoon cubs. Spanish
Description: (Tadpole edition). | Minneapolis, MN : Jump!, Inc., (2018) | Series: Los bebes del bosque | Includes index.
Identifiers: LCCN 2018011209 (print) | LCCN 2018011874 (ebook) | ISBN 9781641280914 (ebook) | ISBN 9781641280907 (hardcover : alk. paper)
Subjects: LCSH: Raccoon—Infancy—Juvenile literature.
Classification: LCC QL737.C26 (ebook) | LCC QL737.C26 N5518 2018 (print) | DDC 599.76/32—dc23
LC record available at https://lccn.loc.gov/2018011209

LOS BEBÉS DEL BOSQUE

LOS KITS

por Genevieve Nilsen

TABLA DE CONTENIDO

Los kits 2

Repaso de palabras 16

Índice 16

tadpole books

LOS KITS

¡Mira! ¡Un kit!

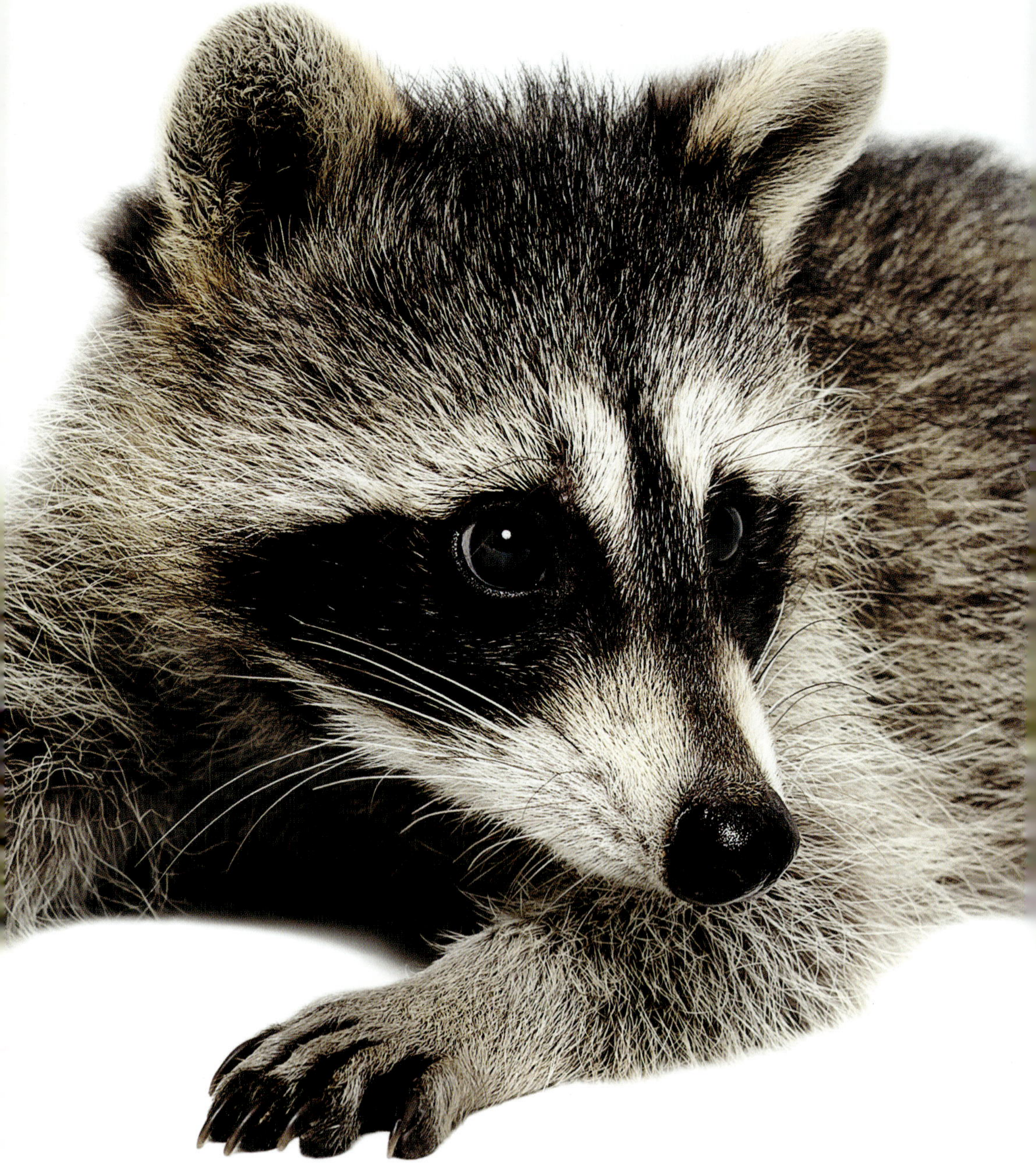

cola

Tiene una cola rayada.

6

máscara

Tiene una máscara.

8

dedo

Tiene dedos.

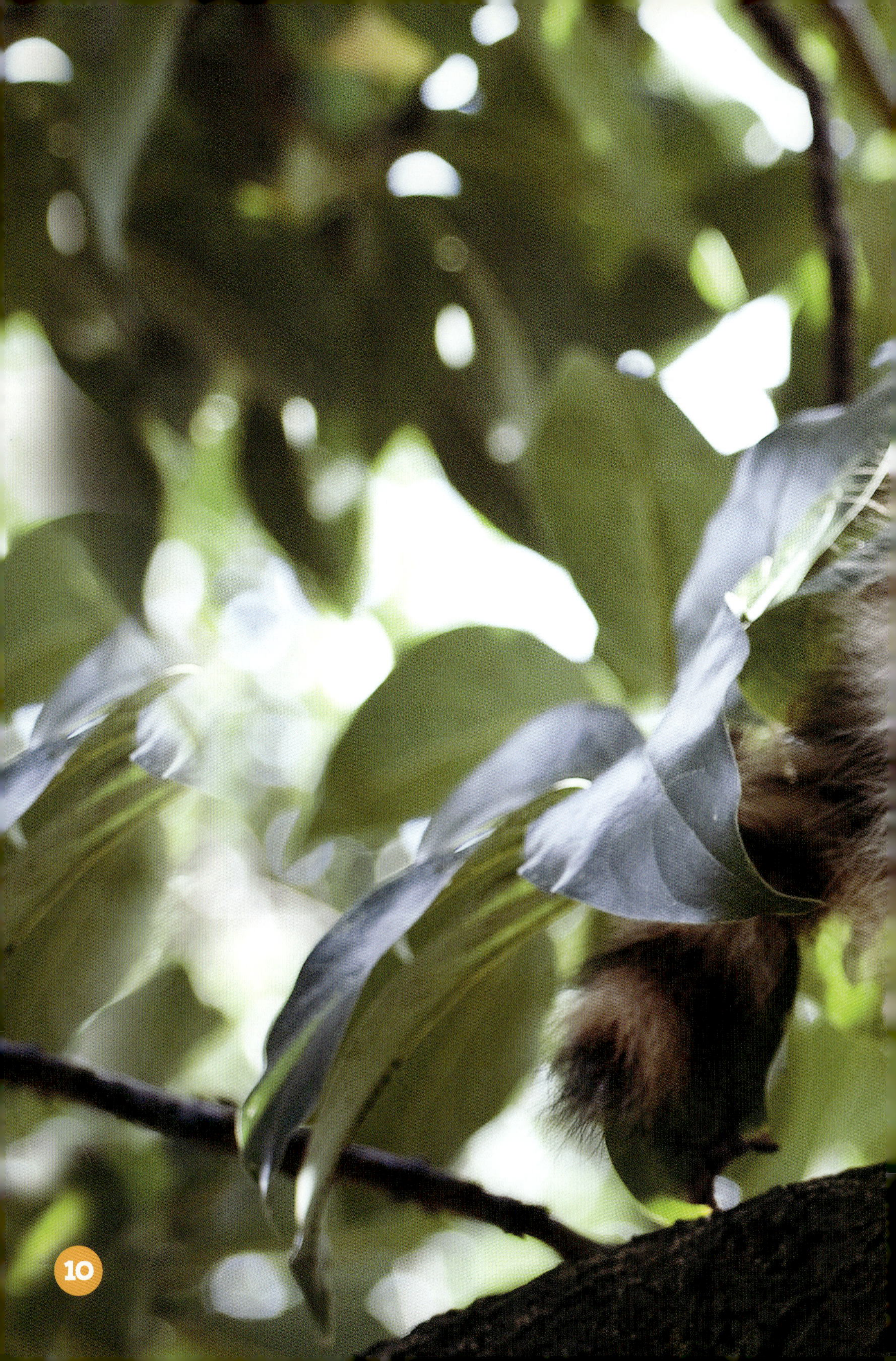

Se trepa.

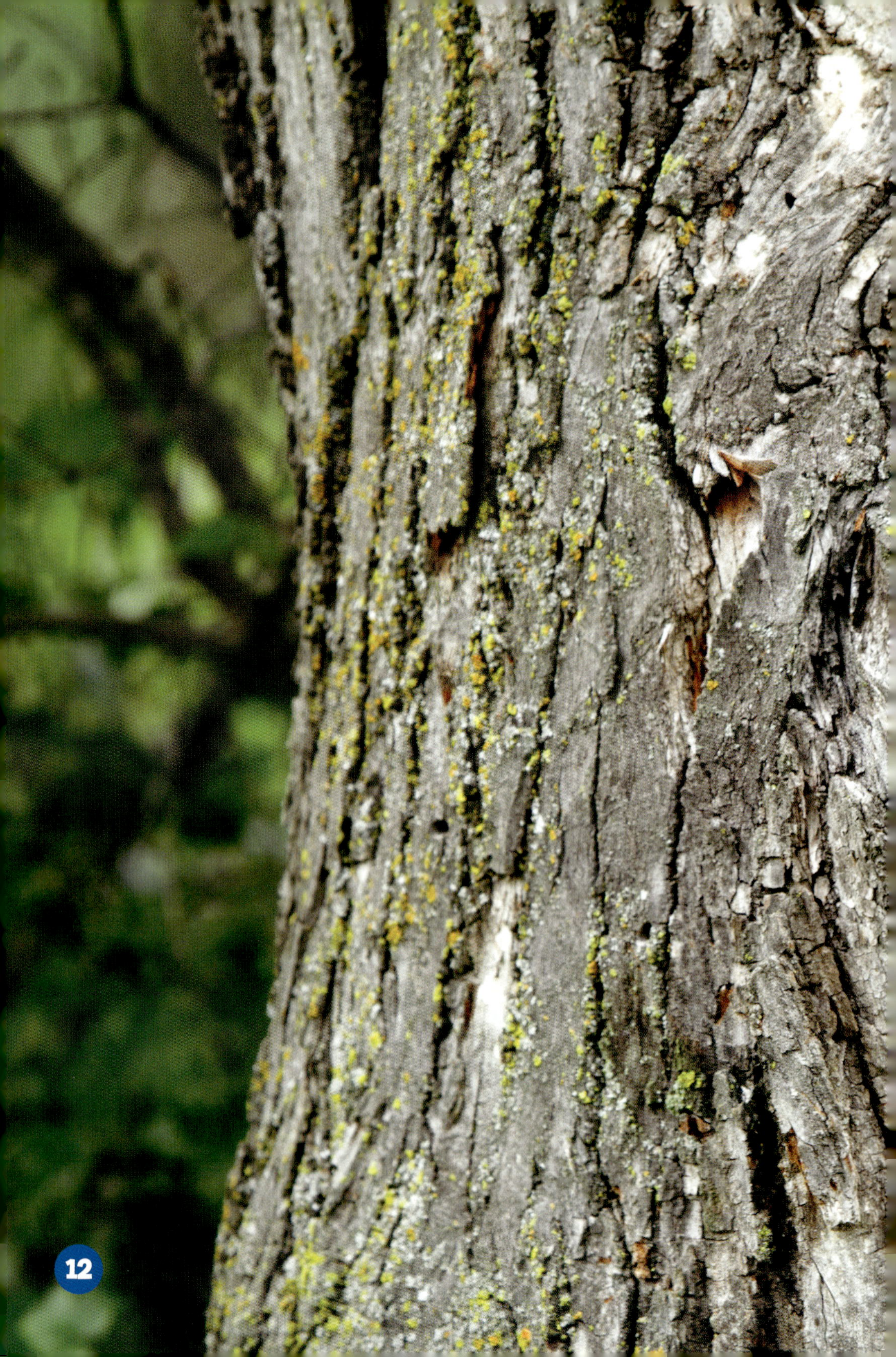

Echa un vistazo hacia afuera.

14

Vive en el bosque.

REPASO DE PALABRAS

bosque

cola

dedos

kit

máscara

se trepa

ÍNDICE

bosque 15
cola 5
dedos 9
echa un vistazo 13

kit 3
máscara 7
se trepa 11
vive 15